T0068291

30 Days To Live

Anntionette Talley

authorHOUSE®

AuthorHouse™
1663 Liberty Drive
Bloomington, IN 47403
www.authorhouse.com
Phone: 1 (800) 839-8640

Published by AuthorHouse 01/27/2017

ISBN: 978-1-5246-5717-8 (sc)
ISBN: 978-1-5246-5716-1 (e)

Library of Congress Control Number: 2016921285

Print information available on the last page.

Preface

This book is dedicated to people just like me, men and women, young and old who have big dreams, who think outside the box. People who think differently, who know you were created for greatness and yet it seems that on many levels you are stuck or there is this invisible brick wall that you cannot get over.

People who life has beat you down and you feel like if you don't do something now you just won't make it. To all the folks who see the glass half full for others but can never quite seem to see that for yourself. Today is your day, this book begins the journey for positive living, self-discovery and your successful future. As I was writing this book I was going through my own healing process and so I made the choice to go through it with you.

Contents

Preface v

Chapter 1: Location 1

Chapter 2: Are you happy? 5

Chapter 3: Absolute stroke of Genius 9

Chapter 4: Casting your pearls before swine 17

Chapter 5: Do you wonder why? 25

Chapter 6: Baby steps....................................31

Chapter 7: Be Kind.. 37

Thank you!... 41

Chapter 1

Location

Before you begin any journey you must first find your current location. By location I do not mean your current physical location; my intention is to evaluate your mental, spiritual and emotional location.

Where are you emotionally? Are you happy, content and at peace or are you angry, disappointed, feeling let down or shorted? Same goes for your mental location and your spiritual location. Now, I do not ask this to make you feel bad nor to judge but I ask you this so that you can see where you are.

The human mind is one of Gods most magnificent creations. It controls all of the functions in your body. On time and on schedule... it has a memory function that far surpasses any computer system. In most cases, in moments of bodily malfunction it runs the healing program long before you even know you are sick or have been infected. There are moments when you have mental strokes of genius and moments when you feel as though you should be in a corner sucking your thumb. On any level we can all agree that the human mind has an awesome ability and purpose.

Did you know that God created you with creative power? That your mind has the ability to think and bring forth change? That within your head is the ability to alter your now and your tomorrow?

What if I told you that within your mind you can move mountains and bring forth your heart's desire. Well you don't have to believe me, I'll prove it: Proverbs 23:7 says for as he thinketh in his heart, so is he: (KJV), yup you read that correctly whatever you are thinking, dwelling on, concentrating on, mentally rehearsing and/or replaying, that is what you are.

Your thoughts are your location! Now take a few moments and think of the dominating thoughts you have thought about just in the last few hours. Whatever you have been concentrating on that is what you have become. The more negative thoughts mean--yes you guessed it, the more negative your reality becomes! For example if you spend your every waking moment thinking about how you don't want to be sick... or even if you don't feel well. At that moment you just keep talking about how you feel sick, chances are if you are not already sick you will be and you will get sicker.

You see, you kept thinking about it and since your mind has the power to create, what you think is what you get! Think of it in terms of your thoughts and your words are seeds, keeping in mind that your words, voice, tongue and thoughts all work together. The words you speak and or listen to are seeds and your heart is the soil and your mind brings about the harvest which your mouth re-seeds. Make sense? Ok, let's look at it this way, if you know anything about grass, you plant the seeds, you nurture it by water and sun and it grows. Good grass when left to mature will grow and produce seeds after its own kind and re-seed itself. So are your realities--you plant good thoughts, positive thoughts in your heart by thinking and speaking good things.

Chapter 2

Are you happy?

Matthew 7:7: *Ask and it shall be given seek and ye shall find, knock and it shall be opened. (KJV)*

I believe that within each of us is a barometer that measures the atmosphere of our lives, it feels the temperature of our destiny, our purpose and our God given creative assignment. Often times we get the discomfort of negating what we are created to do, confused by the negative outlook of our current circumstances. As humans we spend a lot of time being mentally side tracked by what we see before us or the opinions of others about us, taking no thought for what truly fulfills us.

What do you enjoy doing? I mean really truly enjoy, what is that one thing that you could do with joy, with your eyes closed without any thought for the rest of your life without feeling disgruntled or feeling trapped. Nine times out of ten this is your God given assignment in the earth and the ultimate key to your success. It is what you were created to do.

What is success?

Success is defined by the Merriman-Webster dictionary as the fact of achieving wealth, respect or fame: The correct or desired result of an attempt. Simply put if you set out to do something no matter how large or how small the moment you accomplish it you are a success. You have succeeded at accomplishing your goal. Success is just that simple! Now take a few moments and think of all the goals no matter how small or how large you set out to do and you got it done; with that alone you are already long on your way. You are already a successful individual.

Part of what will change your life is pin-pointing your purpose and then going after it. Yes it will take time and it will take effort on your part, but the key to living a successful life is to keep pushing, to keep trying, to never ever give up. I must be honest with you there will be some bumps in the road, there will be challenges, there will be days when you may even get tired but keep pushing know that your goal with each passing moment is within arm's length.

Below I will give you a few starting points to get you started. There will be a more detailed listing closer to the end, but for the sake of not overwhelming you we will start here.

Step one: Get a notebook, write it out. What do you want? Don't be shy if you can dream it you can do it. Write the thought process on how are you going to do it? Remember this is just a starting point.

Step two: Speak it out. Tell the atmosphere what you want and what you are going to do.

Step three: Talk to God about it. Ask Him for direction. Remember ask and it shall be given to you what better way to start an adventure than to request the creator for backing and an instruction manual.

Step four: Get excited about it, think happy thoughts about your upcoming success. Keeping in mind your universe responds to your emotions.

Step five: Dream about it. Allow yourself to dream again, think about all the possibilities of your outcome and the successful nature of your future.

~~~~~~~~

Notes

_____

_____

_____

_____

_____

_____

_____

_____

_____

_____

_____

_____

_____

_____

Chapter 3

Absolute stroke of Genius

Exodus 3:14 we find Moses and God engaged in a conversation. God has just given Moses a seemingly impossible charge, and Moses sees his inadequacy in it. Much like most of the things we face in our lives. Daily we are faced with situations and moments in life where we know they are bigger than us. One morning I was in my bathroom and mentally going over the reflections of the day before when God hit me with a classic. He said "I AM" before I go any further just let that sink in.

When Moses was asking God--- if I may take a moment to paraphrase…"Hey these people don't trust me, and you just want me to waltz up in there and tell these people what you said, and they are supposed to believe me?" "Who shall I tell them sent me?" God's response "tell them, I AM that I AM." That is a powerful statement! God did not waist time thinking or addressing what he was not or what he did not have. He just simply said I AM that I AM. That means everything that He said after that it became a reality and would manifest. There was no shortage in his statement nor a shortage in Gods reality that everything that Moses or the Children of Israel ever needed or wanted would be found in Him. The statement alone is an absolute guarantee that He is and was the all in all.

This particular morning as I was in my quiet time; to be exact the date was June 11, 2016 at 8:10 am it hit me that in Genesis 1:27 God said. "So God created man in his own image, in the image of God created he him, male and female he created them" (KJV) Keep up with me I'm going someplace with this. You are created in the image of God. God gave you an awesome gift that is the **Power** of your words. Your words have power, your words bring life: so much so that God in *Matthew 12:36* warns of the consequences of us using our words carelessly. *Proverbs 18:21* warns us of the power that lays within our words, So much so that it says life and death are in the power of the tongue. Which brings us to the God Factor!

The God Factor

YOU ARE Gods most powerful creation. You are His jewels in the earth and your thoughts and words are the current of the earthly atmosphere. If you think about a body of water the water on top can appear calm and a thing of beauty, but under the surface there is a powerful force at work. The current will push you forward, drag you under or push you to the top; your words possess the same power. So much so that daily the enemy wants to take control of your mind. Once someone has control of your mind they have you; because if they have your mind, they have your words and your words have power. They set things into motion.

Which brings us back to this reality of The God Factor, you are created in His image and you have the ability to give an identity to your problem and your situation.

In recent years there have been a surge in people making positive affirmations, it wasn't until I read a book by Earl Nightingale called *"The Strangest Secret in the World,"* that I truly gained an understanding of this concept. Truly I really never seen the purpose of it until I read the book and God begin to reveal to me about the power of my words and how all my life I had been speaking my own demise or my own failure. The truth is I was broken, mistreated, poor, neglected and unloved because I said I was.

I promise you, every day of my life I had misused or inappropriately used the gift and the power that God had given me called my mouth. Even now when I think back on what I have spoken and the verbal seeds that I have planted--it makes me cringe, and all I can do is pray and declare a crop failure over every negative word that I have ever spoken. Truth is we spend a lot of time in prayer groups praying against curses that we think other people have put on us or praying against evil or the Devil and honestly it is most of us that have done it to ourselves. The power, the God given power, the power of the "I Am" is within you!

What does that mean--that means just as God is, so you are. Now don't get it twisted, I did not say you were God, but he did grant you the power of earthly dominion. He gave you the power to speak something on earth and it be done on earth as it is in heaven; see *Matthew 18:18.* Do you see the power of your words? Heaven and Earth respond to what You say. If you say it, at that very moment it is put into motion. This is why prayer is so important. Jesus tells us in *James 4:2* at the very end of the verse. He said "ye have not because ye ask not." *Matthew 7:7* says "ask and it shall be given" when you go down to verse 8 it says that "everyone that ask receives."

So now me being me, I have always had a thought with God that if you are all seeing and all knowing, all hearing, you are everything to everyone... Why do I have to say or ask for what I want, you already know it before I speak it? I mean after all according to *Psalm 94:11* you know my thoughts, why do I have to speak it? I even went so far as to say me being a writer it was just easier for me to write my prayers. It helped me stay focused and it helped me make sure I covered everything. For a season of my life I found it difficult to even speak my prayers and at times hard to pray. Why because the enemy was after my words, my thoughts, because my words have power and your words have power.

You Sir, and you Lady are created in the image of God and you have been given the charge, authority and power of your words with the understanding that you should use your words wisely.

We have heard a lot of talk about vision in today's time; in churches we have heard repeated messages on Vision, most coming from *Habakkuk 2:2*: write the vision and make it plan upon the tablets. "But know this Vision does not become a reality until you get it out of your head and into the earth in action by your words so that Heaven can back it, orchestrate it and make it manifest be it word on paper or spoken.

So today, now I challenge you to use your words. Speak forth to change your very existence. Say it out loud so that the earth and heaven can have something to work with... speak out what you are believing for, dreaming of and what you stand in need of. Don't hide your dreams and your ambitions anymore. Break out of the prison of your silence. Declare to the elements the arrival of your true purpose of God. Do this often and do this daily until you see the desired results.

2 Corinthians 10:4 tells us" the weapons of our warfare are not carnal or of the flesh--but have divine power to destroy strongholds." Where is your power? It is in your words! The King James Version says they are "for the pulling down of strong holds." Consider this when you speak, where does it go? Your words go out as tiny molecular seeds to bring forth a harvest of what you have requested. Now the funny thing about planting seeds is the soil you are planting in does not discriminate. You can plant flowers or weeds they both will grow. Same is true in the atmosphere. You can verbally plant whatever you like, you can plant the negative or the positive, life or death, success or failure, sickness or health it's all up to you! Today make a choice of what the rest of your days will hold for you. Now for some of you who have thought that everything wrong is from the devil, I will submit this to you -- *James 4:7* says" resist the devil and he will flee". How do you resist something you tell it NO! Use your words. We tell our children when they are small use their words, when someone is angry we ask them to talk to us and to communicate. Deep down inside our spirit man knows the creative power of our words.

Words tell us everything, a person's feelings, their spiritual location, their passion, likes and dislikes. Yes deep down we know the power of our words. IF you say that you don't, I want you to think of the last time someone said something awful to you and it hurt your feelings. Words have power. The words of the parent mold the future of their child. Some of us need to go back and cancel the word assignments that our parents and loved ones have spoken over our lives. Just take a few moments now to think about all the word seeds that were negative that have been planted in your life and take this moment to tell it NO AND YOU ARE CANCELED IN JESUS NAME!

There is power in our words but what good is power unused or used unwisely which brings me back to the God Factor. You have the power to change your world by your words, by what you say. So let's start today, begin by saying I AM_____ and finish this statement with something positive or what you dream of and desire. Keeping in mind that we are what we say we are. So for me it started with I AM an award winning bestselling Author.... And after confessing it daily day after day, heaven and earth took my positive verbal confession and adjusted the universe to make my request become a reality and guess what you are reading my book today. I so desperately wanted to share this life changing, life altering word and lesson with the world. My goal was to reach people just like me, people that have big dreams, great purpose, people that know deep down inside that God has created them for great and big things. People who know they were created to be successful but could not seem to get over the invisible wall that seems to always block them. I am here for the folks that have big dreams but seem to be at a standstill.

Today God has blessed me to be here to help and deliver powerful message to you. You are great, you are successful and today God needs you to use your words!!! I AM_____

Chapter 4

Casting your pearls before swine

"Do not give dogs what is sacred: do not throw your pearls to pigs. If you do they may trample them under their feet and turn and tear you to pieces."
Matthew 7:6

In this life many people will come into your life for many different reasons. Some will come to assist you in your journey and your destiny, and some will come just to encourage you. In the same light, there will be people who are sent solely to distract you and discourage you. There will be people who come acting as if they are there to help but truly are there to highjack the God given vision for your life. Truth is life will bring all kinds of people your way. Heck there will be spectators who won't help or hurt you but will stand on the sidelines and watch you. Yes some will celebrate when you make it, but others are there in their own misery waiting on you to fail purely so they can have something to talk about (but we decree and declare that they will be waiting in vain because you will not fail).

The truth of the matter is "why" they are there really is not the issue. It is the importance of what you do with them while they are in your life, keeping in mind that *Ecclaiastes 3:1* says "to everything there is a season, and a time to every purpose under the heaven" I believe this is true for people and relationships. The people that God sends into your life have a purpose there is no such thing as happenstance. We serve a strategic God, the ultimate General, he is the perfect Chess player. He is a God of purpose and so whatever comes your way, whoever comes your way seek the Father early so that you know why they are there so that you can allow them to fulfill their purpose and not try to keep them past their season. Anything kept past its season will spoil.

The funny thing about season is if you purchase cherries outside of its season yes it is eatable, yes it is still a cherry but you will never get the same benefits of a cheery out of its season that you would get from a cherry in its season. Truth is we must be mindful and pray to God for wisdom on the purpose of people in our lives.

Far too often we give our all --- all of our time, our money and our resources to people who don't value the gift that is within us. We spend countless dollars trying to subconsciously make people like us. We put up with people who if you were where you wanted to be in your life you would not even think twice about having them removed from the space they occupy in your life. You cast your pearls before swine. I bring this up because Success takes dedication, it takes sacrifice and it takes focus and we must be mindful of how we live our daily lives and the resources that God has given us for the task.

What are your pearls? Below are some fine points on what we often overlook or misuse and valuable pearls in our lives:

Pearl 1: *Time*

The most valuable irreplaceable asset you have in this earthly body is time. Once it's gone you cannot get it back. There are no do overs for time what you did 10 minutes ago is done you cannot redo it in that moment.

What and who you give your time to is who holds a part in your future outcomes. Your time is valuable.

Pearl 2: *Your energy*

Your energy and efforts are what you use to fulfill your God given purpose in this earth. If you find yourself exhausting yourself on others and there is nothing left for what God created you to do this is a big problem. How can you accomplish your goals when you have burned out all your oil on counterproductive people and things?

People who do nothing but call you on the phone to complain or gossip without resolve, who appear to just talk just to hear themselves talk. People, who are negative no matter how good things are, people who will always find the bad in every situation. People who seem to show up the very moment you start working on your goals, or have an issue with it or always pop up with something else to do …... They may possibly be Swine.

Pearl 3: *Your Dreams, Goals and Vision*

I will be the first to say you cannot share everything, with everybody. Sometimes the reason why some people hang around you is not because you are cool or awesome. But it's because they are spiritually barren and they are looking for a way to highjack, mimic or steal your spiritual baby.

They are spiritual low or empty or a cracked vessel and in an effort to still shine they will much like a mosquito suck it from you and feed it to others as their own. Leaving you depleted and the virtue they have taken from you tainted. My God, how many dreams of yours have been high jacked…Never again.

Pearl 4: Your Resources

Where your resources are…your money, your time, your energy, that is where you are. Think about this, if you took all your resources and put them into your dreams your God given purpose how far along would you be? To be painfully honest you would probably be a millionaire. Your resources are important, they are provided for the purpose of you accomplishing and completing the vision that you were created to do. Now don't get me wrong this earth still functions off seed time and harvest time. There will come times where you will have to share and give, but in the same token you must be mindful of your resources and be wise with what you have been given.

The sad thing about people that suck up your resources and never appear to give back is that this is a form of greed and greed is never ever satisfied and just like the swine it will suck up every available resource and keep asking, demanding for more and when it is no more it will turn and trample what you hold precious under its feet in the mud and come after you, with the purpose of destruction.

The more you give the more it will want.

I had a season of my life where I had to re-evaluate my relationships with people. I found that in most of my relationships I was the one constantly giving with no return, keeping in mind again that seed time and harvest time are always in effect. I noticed in some relationships I was doing crazy things to keep people happy, even to the partial destruction of myself, health and soul and still they were not satisfied. It was not until I made the decision to cut the tie and disconnect the flow that I was able to see just how evil and selfish the people were.

You have to value your resources and use them only in accordance to the will of God. Truth is, what will the value of a pearl be to a pig anyway? It has no value to a pig it just wants what you have.

Pearl 5: *Your Heart*

This one is one of the most readily given and quickly destroyed. A broken heart is the most life altering experience there is and yet we give it so carelessly.

Your heart in the wrong hands can bring such a powerful ripple in the earth that the effects will be felt for centuries to come, you don't believe me? Have you ever known a person who was single and without them saying you knew someone new had come into their life? Their heart had been altered.

Have you ever been working on a project with a person and they became frustrated with it and they became hard to work with, their heart had changed or someone new to the faith and they are full of joy; their heart has changed.

Where and what you give your heart to will eventually become your everything. In that moment it becomes the most important thing in your world. Your heart is valuable don't just give it to any old thing.

Pearl 6: *You: you are the vessel created for change in the earth*.

God values you enough to want to dwell in you. So you... Vessel are priceless. You cannot afford to just put you in all kinds of risky situations. You are important, you are valuable. This world needs you and what you have to offer the earth needs you. That is why you are here, you have purpose.

Don't waste your purpose and deny God the vessel and the pearl God called you to be, because this world has nothing more in mind but to break you.

Pearl 7: *Your word!*

There used to be a saying that said "my word is my bond"--- old folks use to say you are only as good as your word. If you say it do it, but I caution you to be mindful before you speak. Too often our mouths write checks our behinds cannot cash. We make vows or promises or commitments to people and things that will draw us away from our destiny.

Don't be so quick to speak. The bible says in *James 1:19* "be slow to speak and quick to listen."

Some folks want you to talk so they can have something to talk about. Ask God to deliver you from the urge to have mindless chatter. Remember you will be judged on every idle word. Watch your pearls they are of value.

All of these pearls are of value and all of them hold a part in your destiny. Stop just throwing them on the ground. The more you give the more the swine will want and eventually it will come after you. Save and use your pearls wisely.

~~~~~~~~

Chapter 5

Do you wonder why?

Transfer!! **Proverbs 13:22** ... *the wealth of the wicked is laid up for the just. (KJV)*

There is a wealth transfer on the horizon.

Failure is not an option: Do this, because there is nothing left to do, you have tried everything else, and it has left you in a place of discontent. You tried complaining about your discontentment. How far did you get with that one? You tired ignoring the issue, when you turned around there it was still waiting for you. Some have tried drugs, drinking and sex to cover up their discontentment with their current situation only to find themselves unhappy.

It has been said that the definition of insanity is to do the same thing over and over again the same way and expect a different result. The old folks use to say it's a poor wind that does not change. Truth is if you want something different you are going to have to change your mind, change your way of thinking. Even the bible tells us in *Romans 12:2* to renew our minds daily. So I ask you this. If day after day your circumstances and your outlook are still the same are you truly renewing your mind? Change starts in your mind!

To change your life you have to change your mind. Reject negative thoughts, reject depression, reject failure, reject lack, reject poverty and reject sickness. Reject every negative thought and aspect of your life. Reject! Reject! Reject!

The bible says in *James 4:7* resist the devil and he will flee. Don't you see how powerful you are, how powerful your words are, how powerful your thoughts are. For some of us we need to take this a step further the bible says in *Philippians 3:13(KJV)* "forgetting those things which are behind us and pressing towards the mark of the high calling."

The stuff in your past, forget about it, who hurt you forget about it, who did or did not do something forget about it. Do not ever allow the hurts of your past to hinder you from the glory of your spectacular future.

Have you ever tried to run a race with a truck, a bus and an airplane tied to your waist? Seems pretty silly doesn't it, just the thought of it, you almost have to laugh at the visual don't you? Well truth is we do this every single day (well we did) we try to run this race called life with destiny and success being the finish line with every weight from our past tied around our waist. You have become weighted down, exhausted, tired, frustrated because you are letting who you were get in the way or hinder who you are and who you will become.

Stop letting what was stop you from what you were created to be. You are more than a conqueror through Christ Jesus (*Romans 8:37*). You have overcome by the blood of the lamb (*Revelation 12:11*). You are not who they said you were, you are not a failure, you are not ugly, you are not useless, or stupid you are not a statistic or whatever negative seeds the world has tried to plant in your life. You are fearfully and wonderfully made (*Psalm 139:14*) you are the apple of Gods eye (*Zechariah 2:8*) and guess what? You are right on track to achieve your God given destiny, healing has come to you here in the earth that is why I am writing this book and why you have it in your hands.

As a matter of fact stop right now and repeat after me:

> *I am the righteousness of Christ!*
> *I am important!*
> *I am necessary!*
> *I am great!*
> *I am every good thing God says I am!*
> *I am divinely made for a divine and appointed purpose!*
> *I am somebody!*

Repeat it if you have to, scream it if you have to. If you have to say it through tears then let the tears flow. But know this never again will you ever be the same, never again will you bare the wounds of what the past tried to label you with. Every time the past tries to stamp you again, you reject it. Stop letting life tell you who you are, you tell life who you are. The mind can be one heck of a battle ground but you were equipped to win it. You were created to win it. Remember God is not in the business of losing or being embarrassed. So if you are in it, you had better believe he intends on you winning the fight.

We see in *Job 1:7-13* we see Job minding his own business doing everything he knows to get it right with God. And God makes the suggestion to the enemy of His name.

Now this really made me question some things, my own thoughts, my own beliefs and I had to inquire God. God you know the enemy meant him no good, you know his desire was to destroy him. He told you he wanted to destroy him. And God spoke to me ever so sweetly and said I did it because I trusted him "I trusted that he would rather die than to curse me" "I trusted him" that statement rocked me to my core.

For many of you, you were in what you were in, you were born into the family you were born into because out of the entire world of all of the earth's people God trusted you! You... you ... God trusted you the God of all creation, of all the universe trusted you not to let him down or turn on him ... The amazing Deity trusted you to not to let him down. I cannot stress this enough; the Almighty God maker of the Heavens and earth trusted you with the situation you are in and have come through and overcome. Let that sink in for a moment.....

You may be asking yourself how can you say that. Because you are still here you are reading this book, you have overcome because you are not dead you are still alive. And if the Almighty God trusts you with what you are going through he will not allow you to fail. God will not have it, you will be ok, you will be better than ok, you will succeed! There are more for you than can ever be against you. Failure is not an option you were created for success. You were created to succeed and accomplish your God given destiny. Say it with me I was chosen, handpicked by God to get this done, I am created to succeed, I will not fail, failure is not an option for me. There is a transfer of Good things, awesome things in this life and the transfer of it is already ordained for me!

~~~~~~~

Notes

_____

_____

_____

_____

_____

_____

_____

_____

_____

_____

_____

_____

_____

_____

_____

_____

_____

_____

_____

_____

Chapter 6

Baby steps

Rome was not built in a day! I have heard this saying all of my life and never really understood it until now. Most times after reading a book like this we get all amped up and excited and ready to take the world by storm only to get overwhelmed and frustrated when we start the process and it does not go as quickly as we imagined it should.

Life changes take time. It takes 9 months for a baby to become completely formed, it has taken years for you to get to the point that you are at now. So to lessen the frustration I have found that it is easiest to eat the pizza one slice at a time.

Step One: The first step in this process is deciding what it is you want to do! Nothing is too silly or too farfetched. If you can think it or dream it you can do it! So let's start here, you will need something to write with and something to write on. My first stroke of genius was written on toilet paper but for me it was just that important that I had to get it out at that moment.

Step Two: Write it down! Write down what it is that you desire: there are no limitations here, just remember to dream big and be honest with yourself. In this moment the thoughts and opinions of others do not exist. Be true to yourself on this one. Don't be fearful what you write today is just a starting point and as you progress it will change over time. That shows growth, maturity and that you are settling into your new reality. *Habakkuk2:2* says write the vision and make it plain. Write it down clearly and just how you want it. Be specific and be precise.

Step Three: Say it! Speak it out into the atmosphere, I suggest that every day you say it as many times a day as it takes for you to start believing that you can do it, will do it and have done it. This will condition your mind to understand that you are going for this and you will get it. Plant the seeds of positivity in your own mind for the goal you have set for yourself. During my process every time I would face opposition or something that was contrary to what I was believing for or working towards I would just keep repeating my new reality until my emotions got the message. Remember. *Job 22:28(KJV)* says "thou shalt also decree a thing and it shall be established unto thee."

Step Four: Pray, pray, and pray some more; talk to God about it, what good is a plan and goal if you leave out the one who can make it happen? Remember *Matthew 7:7* tells us to ask and it shall be given. Open your mouth and ask for it! Far too often we just breeze by this scripture. God was very clear he said "ask and it shall be given" He is your Dad just like when children come to their parents and ask for something as a parent you find a way to make sure your child gets what they need to fulfill their purpose in the earth. The same is your Father in heaven, just ask.

Step Five: Get excited about it, visualize it, and began to See it. *Mark 9:23* says "if thou can believe, all things are possible to him that believes" you have got to believe it. No matter what everything around you looks like you have got to believe it and in believing in it, believing in you, get excited about it. If you have ever had a crush on someone you know the feeling you get when you think of him or her that giddy feeling you get? That's how you should feel when you think of your goals. You should feel like you are already experiencing it. Don't worry sometimes this takes time but keep saying it until you can feel it.

Remember your emotions are powerful, tame them for your benefit.

Step Six: Dream about it! Dreaming is a form of Visualization, your dreams are your vision for your life, start dreaming again. Day dream about it, take time out your day and dedicate it to the mental conditioning of your future. See yourself in that car, in the bank line taking out your fortune, you got to see it for yourself.

When you begin this journey, well…when I began my journey I was very secretive about it, for me I could not mentally afford to have people telling me what I could not do and what was impossible. Remember their reality is not your reality. You are here to do what you were created to do. But as I went through the process eventually I found myself strong enough to share some things and then God gave me courage to defend my vision. So it is a judgement call that only you can make weather to share your dream or not, but whatever you decided keep dreaming.

Step Seven: Let's make some moves: Start making steps no matter how big or small to live it, study up on it, ask about it, Read books of inspiration, read the Bible, and look at YouTube videos on success. Whatever you are most comfortable with just start taking steps towards your goal. My first steps were just writing my thoughts on tissue, in note books, in my Phone. Talking in the mirror as if I was standing on a stage speaking on the subject that I knew God had given me.

Then as I made small steps, God would gave me the courage to make bigger ones then I did a YouTube video, then a periscope video. Then I prayed some more and now you are reading the results of my persistence. Whatever your dream is stick with it, push for it and keep moving in its direction. You have a destiny to meet!

Last: Take the time: as with any new adventure it takes time and dedication, take the necessary time, the title of this book is *30 days to Live*! Take this adventure 30 days at a time. Take the 1st 30 days and repeat each step daily, and if need be take another 30 days and another until you have reached your goal. The important thing here is not to give up, to push through. Knowing that you can do this!

~~~~~~~~

Notes

_____

_____

_____

_____

_____

_____

_____

_____

_____

_____

_____

_____

_____

_____

_____

_____

_____

_____

_____

_____

_____

_____

_____

_____

_____

_____

_____

_____

_____

Chapter 7

Be Kind

I dare not end this book without giving you the knowledge of seed time and harvest time. You are only as good as you are to others. This book is by no means a license to be selfish or cruel to others while you are trying to reach your goals. My Mother always told me "those same folks you see on the way up, you will see on the way down" another favorite saying of hers "that same person you mistreat may one day have to give you a glass of water" In chapter 4 we dealt with people with swine like mentalities--people who most likely are abusive or just toxic to your life. In this chapter we will deal with the people that God has placed in your life as a means for you to plant good seeds into, keeping in mind that we are all in this thing together. We are the human race, there is room for all in this earth and we were all created equal.

In this life you are only as good as you are to others, this book although it is about you and your goals again and I cannot express this strongly enough it's not intended as a permission slip to be selfish or mean if that is your goal you are doing it all wrong. We only get back what we have put out. There is no way you can accomplish your dream alone. You will need some help! With that being said I am a firm believer in you draw to you what you send out from you.

If you need kindness and mercy then you will have to give kindness and mercy. Let love be the banner that people see in you, yes you will be wise with your resources and your vision. But in the same token this is not the time to be putting out any negative energy.

So smile because you are going someplace in this life, be at peace because you have been handpicked by God to do what you have been dreaming about forever. One day in my prayer time God revealed to me that my vision was in fact His vision for me that was why I could never let it go. This should be a journey of fulfillment. If you find yourself being anxious or frustrated you are going about it wrong. Remember this is a process, it takes time, it takes faith, it will take resources but it will also take people to make it happen.

So during this season of growth, be positive, be kind, and be loving. There will be times when you will need to be a blessing to someone else, do it knowing that the greatest success of any human being is the success of being kind to a fellow brother or sister.

It is my prayer that just like me through this book that you will realize that you were created for greatness, that your dreams are real and are ready to become a reality. You are somebody and nothing can hold you back! You are created in the image of God and He has given you a power that is without limit or measure, you have the power of your words, thoughts, dreams and a new understanding that your reality is now. Who you were yesterday no longer exist today you are a new you and from you will come great things.

****

Notes

_____

_____

_____

_____

_____

_____

_____

_____

_____

_____

_____

_____

_____

_____

_____

_____

_____

_____

_____

_____

_____

_____

_____

_____

_____

_____

_____

Thank you!

I just wanted to say a special thank you to each reader for taking this challenge and life changing journey with me. We are about to take this world by storm. I also wanted to say thank you to all my family and friends for all the encouragement that you have given me to get me to this point. Thank you to my Mom for your love, sound wisdom and for always being in my corner. Thank you to my sister Felicia for always being my cheerleader. My brother Jay for being there for whatever, Norvell for always having my back. Thank you to all of my family, my Detroit Eviction Defense family words cannot express my thankfulness. Thank you to my heart, my world my children My princess Ashley you are my strength, my Prince Willis you are my joy and my grandbaby Arthur you are my joy. I love you all today, tomorrow and forever. Thank you to my team Shamekia Little I promise you God could not have sent me a better angel, sister and editor thank you for all your love, time effort and encouragement. To the first lady of the RUG movement Kellie Henderson thank you for being my backbone in this and for keeping me grounded and being down for whatever and keeping me beautiful. I just wanted to thank everyone that played their part in this to my MLK family and babies I love y'all so much to my Crockett babies y'all have my heart. I know I did not have room to put every name here but I promise you my heart and heaven know your name and I have thanked God daily for you. Thank you to Donnathon Dobson for blessing me with such an awesome book cover your work still stirs my heart. Most importantly thank you God for choosing me, for loving me and for making me special. Truly you had a better plan (Courtesy of Rev Brittene Harper).

Printed in the United States
By Bookmasters